WOW!
AMAZING FACTS ABOUT
ANIMALS

This edition published by Parragon Books Ltd in 2016

Parragon Books Ltd
Chartist House
15–17 Trim Street
Bath BA1 1HA, UK
www.parragon.com

ISBN 978-1-4748-5060-5

Printed in China

WOW!

AMAZING FACTS ABOUT ANIMALS

PaRRagon

Bath • New York • Cologne • Melbourne • Delhi
Hong Kong • Shenzhen • Singapore

10 FACTS ABOUT APES

Apes are large primates with no tails and big brains. **Humans are a species of ape.** #001

Newborn chimps have a tuft of white fur **on their bottoms.** #002

The name 'orang-utan' means 'person of the forest' in Malay. #004

Families of gibbons **SING SONGS** together while they sit in the trees. #003

Chimpanzees
and bonobos are the closest relatives of humans. #005

CHIMPS are poor swimmers, but they do wade through **SHALLOW WATER.** They hold their arms above their heads as they do so. #007

The orang-utan is the **largest fruit-eating animal** in the world. #006

4

Mountain gorillas live in the high mountains of central Africa. They have **extra-thick fur** to keep them warm. #008

GORILLAS are the largest **PRIMATES.** #009

An adult male can weigh **200 KILOGRAMS** – that's heavier than two adult humans. #010

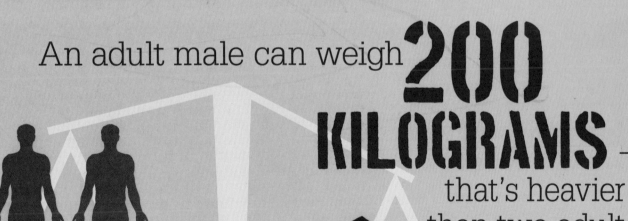

7 FACTS ABOUT Cats

Cats have much better **night vision** than humans. We need **six times** more light to see as clearly as a cat.

#001

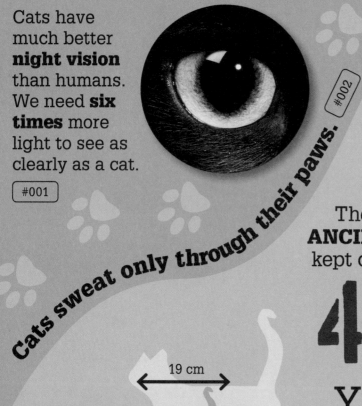

#002

Cats sweat only through their paws.

Cats purr when they are ill. The vibrations may help their bones and muscles to heal.

#003

The **ANCIENT EGYPTIANS** kept cats as pets nearly

4000 YEARS AGO.

#004

19 cm

7 cm

The **smallest adult cat ever measured** was a **Himalayan-Persian** called **Tinker Toy,** which was only **7 centimetres** tall and **19 cm** long – about the size of a rat.

#005

There are currently

55

recognized **breeds** of house cat.

#006

Cats sometimes **chew grass** to make themselves **throw up fur balls.**

#007

6 BIG CAT FACTS

The **cheetah** is the **fastest land mammal,** and can accelerate from **0 to 95 kilometres per hour** in just 3 seconds. That's the same as an F1 racing car. #001

Most **jaguars** are orange with black spots, but about **6 per cent** are black all over. #002

A lion's **ROAR** can be heard from **8 km** away. #003

Tigers are known to imitate the sounds of other animals to lure in prey. #004

Tigers now inhabit only 7 per cent of the area that they lived in **100 years ago,** because humans are taking over their land. #005

LIONS do most of their **HUNTING** at night. #006

7

12 DOG FACTS

Mongol ruler Kublai Khan kept **5000** dogs. #001

Domestic dogs walk in a circle before they lie down, as their wild ancestors would have done to flatten the ground. #002

Greyhounds have been recorded **running at 72 km/h** – that's nearly twice as fast as top human sprinters. #003

A Dalmatian puppy is born completely white. The first spots appear after about three weeks. #004

All dogs have a see-through third eyelid that gives their eyes extra protection. #005

Puppies are born blind, deaf and toothless. #006

A dog's sense of smell is up to

100,000

times more sensitive than a human's. #007

A dog's wet nose traps chemicals in the air, helping it to smell them. #008

Dogs have 18 muscles in their ears. #009

Dogs drink water by forming the back of their tongue into a cup to scoop the water up. #010

The tallest dog is the Great Dane. The biggest of all, called Zeus, stood **1.12 m** from **paw to shoulder** – as tall as an average five-year-old child. #011

About ⅓ of all homes in the world have a pet dog. That's about

half a billion

doggie homes. #012

10 ELEPHANTS
FACTS ABOUT

There are **two kinds** of elephant: **African** and **Asian.** African elephants have much bigger ears. Their big ears keep them cool on hot days. #001

Just as we are left- or right-handed, elephants are left- or right-tusked. The dominant tusk is usually more worn down than the other. #002

Female African elephants have a gestation (pregnancy) that lasts **22 months** – longer than any other animal. #003

Elephants use mud or sand as sun block. #004

Elephants have **26 teeth**, which are usually replaced **6 or 7 times in their life.** They eat plants, and wear their teeth out through chewing. #005

Elephants lift and spread their ears to signal to other elephants when they are alarmed. #006

An elephant's heart beats only **25 times per minute** – about three times more slowly than the average human heart. #007

Female elephants spend all their lives with their family group. **Each group is led by an old female called the matriarch.** #008

An African elephant's trunk is about **2 m long.** #009

Elephants can communicate by **stamping on the ground.** Other elephants sense the vibrations many kilometres away. #010

9 FACTS ABOUT HIPPOS

The name 'hippopotamus' means **HORSE OF THE RIVER** in Greek. #001

An **adult** hippo can weigh more than **3 tonnes** – as much as a medium-sized **elephant**. #003

Hippo milk is **bright pink**. #002

A hippo's eyes are covered with a special clear membrane. The **membrane acts like goggles** to help the hippo see underwater clearly. #004

Nearly **3000** people are **killed by hippos** every year. #005

Hippo skin is **15 CM THICK**. #006

The closest living relatives to hippos are actually **whales**. #007

Its **HUGE** canine teeth are used for **fighting**, **not eating**. #008

Hippos can **sleep underwater**. They bob up to the surface every few minutes to take a breath **without waking up**. #009

5 RHINO
FACTS

Rhinoceroses can grow up to **3.5 m long** – as long as two adult humans lying toe to toe. #002

There are only around **40** JAVAN RHINOS **left on the planet.** #003

Rhinos are very rare because humans hunt them. Nearly

700

were killed in South Africa in 2012.

#004

Rhinos welcome oxpecker birds because they **eat the itchy parasites** that live on the rhino's skin. #001

A rhino's **horn** is made from keratin, the same stuff that our fingernails and hair are made from.

#005

9 FACTS ABOUT BEARS

During late summer and early autumn, GRIZZLY BEARS EAT CONTINUOUSLY **without getting full.** They eat as much as they can to get fat for the winter. #001

All bears share the same ancestor – the dawn bear, which lived more than 20 million years ago. #002

The **spectacled** bear gets its name from the **circular marks** around its eyes, which make it look like it is **wearing spectacles.** #003

The brown bear is the **largest and heaviest** of all bears, weighing as much as **1 tonne** – the weight of a small car. #004

Female grizzly bears can lose **40 per cent** of their body weight over the winter. #005

Over a short distance, a grizzly bear can **outrun a horse.**

#006

Sun bears **love honey.**

They will rip open tree trunks...

...in search of **beehives.**

#007

Polar bears are very strong swimmers, and have been seen more than **100 km** from land.

#008

Grizzly bears usually give birth to

TWINS.

The cubs will stay with their mother for **two years** before going off on their own.

#009

MAMMALS FACTFILE

BIG AND SMALL

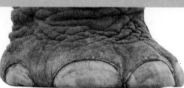

Elephants are the **LARGEST** land mammals. They can weigh over **6 tonnes** but spread their weight over **four large feet,** so they barely leave footprints. #002

The SMALLEST mammal is the bumblebee bat, which weighs just 2 g – the weight of a small coin. #001

A walrus's tusks may be up to **1 M LONG.** #003

An adult giraffe's legs alone are about 1.8 m long – **taller than most humans.** #004

WARM AND HIDDEN

Mammals are all **warm-blooded.** #005

Sloths move so **SLOWLY** that algae grow on their fur. The green algae help to hide the sloths in the trees. #006

During a cold year, a dormouse will stay asleep for more than **6 months.** #007

A polar bear appears white from a distance, but its hairs are transparent. #008

Prairie dogs live in a network of underground tunnels called **a town.** A prairie dog town can cover an area of 100 hectares – **as big as a human town.** #009

The Weddell seal spends most of its life under the sea ice in Antarctica. It keeps breathing holes in the ice open by gnawing the ice away with its teeth. #010

REPRODUCTION

The Virginia opossum has a gestation period of just **12 days**. #013

MAMMALS are the only animals that produce milk. #011

All mammals have **HAIR** when they are born. #012

A newborn panda is SMALLER than a mouse. #014

WEIRD BUT TRUE

BADGERS POO in special latrines some way from **their setts.** #016

In New Zealand there are about **7 sheep** to every person. #017

Some species of shrew are **poisonous.** #015

An elephant's trunk contains **40,000** muscles. #018

HYENAS have huge hearts, making up about **10** per cent of their body weight. #019

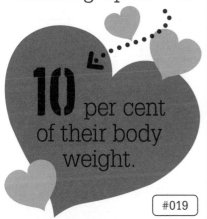

A hyena's bite is so **strong** that it can **CRUNCH** through elephant bones. #020

11 FACTS ABOUT SHARKS

Sharks can detect a single drop of **blood** in an Olympic-sized swimming pool full of **water.**
#001

The smallest shark is the **dwarf lanternshark.** It is just **20 cm** long. #002

THE WHALE SHARK is the biggest fish in the world, growing up to 12 m long – 60 times longer than the dwarf lanternshark. #003

A shark's **skeleton** is made of **bendy cartilage** (the same stuff your nose is made from), **not bone.** #004

If a shark **stops** swimming, it **sinks,** as it does not have a swim bladder to help with buoyancy. #005

SHARKS have been swimming in the oceans for **400 MILLION** years – since before the dinosaurs. #006

A **GREAT HAMMERHEAD** shark's eyes are **1 m** apart. #007

A great white's bite is **three times** more **powerful** than the bite of a **lion.**

#008

On average, fewer than **ten people**

a year are killed by great whites... but more than 1000 people a year are killed by **bees.**

#009

#010

A **GREAT WHITE** shark needs to eat **11 TONNES** of food a year – equivalent in weight to 150 people.

#011

8 MIGHTY WHALE FACTS

Bowhead whales can live for up to **200 years** – the longest lifespan of any mammal. #001

Humpback whales **sing to each other**. A humpback whale's song can be heard by other humpback whales **thousands of kilometres away**. #002

Sperm whales have **no sense of smell**. #003

SPERM WHALE

Sperm whales **dive** to depths of **up to 3 km** in search of food. #004

Sperm whales **feed on giant squid**. The whales often have scars from battles with the squid. #005

20

BOWHEAD WHALE

The bowhead whale has the **largest mouth of any animal**. It measures **up to 4 m** from top to bottom when open.

#006

Unlike other whales, the beluga whale has a **flexible neck** that allows it to turn its head in all directions.

#007

BELUGA WHALE

HUMPBACK WHALE

The male narwhal has a **sword-like spiral tusk** that grows up to 2.7 m long.

#008

NARWHAL

14 facts about CORAL REEFS
and the fish that live in them

Coral looks like a plant, but is actually a simple kind of animal.

#001

Reefs build up over time from the hard skeletons of dead coral.

#002

Reefs grow a few centimetres each year. Some of the largest began growing **50 million years ago.**

#003

Reefs get their vivid colours not from the coral, but from the algae that live with them. #004

Coral likes water that is 26–27°C. If the water is warmer than this, the coral dies. Global warming is a danger to many reefs.
#005

Coral Reef Creatures

When threatened, a puffer fish will fill itself with water, and balloon up to several times its normal size.
#006

When a starfish loses one of its arms, it grows a new one. #007

After mating, the male seahorse carries the eggs in a special pouch until they are ready to hatch. #008

Clownfish live alongside anemones in coral reefs. The anemone provides the fish with food, while the fish protects the anemone from predators.
#009

Coral is very sensitive to pollution. Dirty water kills it.
#010

The Great Barrier Reef

It is the largest coral reef system in the world. It is 2300 km long – two-thirds of the distance from New York to Los Angeles. #011

It contains 2900 individual reefs. #012

It also contains more than 900 islands. #013

It is so big, it can be seen from space. #014

LIFE IN THE SEA
FACTFILE

INCREDIBLE OCEAN

For the first **3 BILLION** years of life on **EARTH**, living things were only found in the oceans. #001

We have only explored **1 PER CENT** of the ocean floor. Many more species of marine animal wait to be discovered. #002

We know more about the **SURFACE OF MARS** than we do about the **ocean floor**. #003

The **oceans** cover **71 per cent** of the planet. #004

REPRODUCTION

SALMON return from the ocean to the river they were born in to spawn. #005

Many fish will **change sex during their lives.**

FISH LAY THEIR EGGS in the Sargasso Sea because the dense seaweed protects their young from predators such as **tuna** or **sea birds.** #006

Sea squirts can **REPRODUCE** by budding. The young **grow out** of the side of the adult's body. #007

#008

MARINE **BODIES**

A giant squid's eyes are **30 cm across** – the size of a dinner plate. #009

When threatened, a sea cucumber may **squirt** out some of its internal organs from its bottom. It later **regrows its missing body parts.** #010

Sea turtles have **special glands** that remove salt from the seawater they drink. #011

A manatee has **whiskers** that it uses like cutlery, to grasp and take in food. #012

SOME STARFISH

eject their stomach to cover and digest prey before pulling it back in. #013

The mantis shrimp has the best eyesight of any animal. Its eyes have **eight different kinds of colour sensor,** compared to three in the human eye. #014

WEIRD BUT TRUE

A lobster's teeth are in its stomach. #015

SPONGES

have the simplest body structure of any animal. #017

The **Pompeii worm** lives around hot vents on the ocean floor. It can survive in temperatures **up to 80°C.** #016

The **right whale** #018

was given its name by whalers because it is slow-moving and easy to hunt.

The **deepest** fish ever found was a cusk eel, which was dredged from the bottom of the Puerto Rico Trench, 8368 m down. #019

Sailors

once thought that the 15-m-long oarfish was a man-eating sea monster. #020

76 brilliant BIRD facts

There are about 10,000 species of bird. [#001] Birds have hollow bones that help them fly. [#002] Around 20 per cent of birds migrate long distances every year. [#003] **Green herons** will sometimes drop an insect in water, then catch the fish that eats the bug. [#004] **Crows** recognize human faces. [#005] They will attack people who have previously attacked them or a crow they know. [#006] Migrating crows will change their route to avoid a place where crows have previously been shot. [#007] In Japan, crows have learned to drop nuts at pedestrian crossings – passing cars crush the shells, and the crows wait for the green light to walk out and eat them in safety. [#008] **Scrub jays** pretend to hide their food if they know other scrub jays are watching, but they will

In many species of bird, only the male has colourful feathers. [#009]

The **peacock** fans his tail feathers to attract mates. [#010]

His feathers can grow to more than 1 m long. [#011]

They fall out and grow again each year. [#012]

really be taking it somewhere else. [#013] **Flamingos** can live in a variety of habitats, even salt lakes. [#014] Special glands near their beaks can filter out excess salt as they feed. [#015] **Malachite kingfishers** bash the heads of fish they have caught against tree trunks to kill them. [#016] The brightly coloured **macaw** birds mate for life. [#017] An **African grey parrot** has displayed an ability to think equivalent to that of a four-year-old child. [#018] The parrot was called Alex. [#019] When he was tired, Alex would give wrong answers on purpose to make tests (to measure his intellect) stop. [#020] The **toco toucan** is the largest of all toucans. [#021] Its bill makes up a third of its length. [#022] A **vulture's** head and neck are bald or covered in short feathers. [#023] This allows it to reach deep inside dead bodies as it feeds. [#024] On a hot day, vultures pee on their legs. [#025] This helps to cool them down. [#026] When a vulture feels threatened, it vomits. [#027] Up to six different species of vulture may feed on the same carcass. [#028] Each will feed on a different part of the body. [#029] Vultures have excellent eyesight. [#030] They can spot a dying animal on the ground several kilometres away. [#031] The wingspan of the **Andean condor** can be as long as 3.2 m. [#032] Each wing is as long as an average adult human. [#033] The condor uses its huge wings to soar high into the air on rising air currents. [#034] It can reach heights of over 4,000 m. [#035] Condors have one chick every other year. [#036] It takes them a whole year to rear the chick. [#037] A male **barn owl** will bring a female a gift of a dead mouse in an effort to win her affections. [#038] At night, male **nightingales** sing to impress the females. At dawn, they sing to defend their territories. [#039] The male **bowerbird** builds a display using twigs and brightly coloured objects to impress females. [#040] Male **frigatebirds** have giant red pouches under their bills that inflate to attract a mate. [#041] **Wandering albatrosses** incubate their eggs for 78 days. [#042] 24 hens' eggs could fit into one **ostrich** egg. [#043] The European **blue tit** lays up to 16 eggs in one clutch. [#044] **Ospreys** lay three eggs, but the eggs do not hatch at the same time. The chick that hatches first is most likely to survive. [#045] Every autumn the **bar-tailed godwit** flies from

Alaska to New Zealand, a distance of 11,000 km. #046 The godwit does this journey in eight days and flies non-stop without a break. #047 They build up fat reserves before the journey to use for energy as they fly. #048 The **Arctic tern** starts its long journey from the Arctic to Antarctica after breeding each year. #049 On the journey south, they stop for a while in the Azores to feed. #050 The terns do not fly straight but follow an S-shaped route – this allows them to take advantage of prevailing winds. #051 Iron-rich blood cells have been found in the tops of **homing pigeons'** beaks. #052 Homing pigeons often follow roads on the ground as they fly home. #053 They even turn off at junctions! #054 During World War II, some aircraft carried pigeons on board. Airmen would send a message home attached to the pigeons if their planes were shot down. #055 Homing pigeons use the position of the sun to help them navigate. #056 Eyesight is the most important sense for birds. Their vision is two to three times more detailed than humans'. #057 Most birds have a poor sense of taste and smell. #058 **Oilbirds** live in dark caves and use echolocation to find their way around. #059 Weighing in at up to 18 kg, male **korl bustards** and **great bustards** share the record for the heaviest flying birds. #060 **Rüppell's griffon vulture** is possibly the highest flyer, climbing to over 10,000 m. #061 The **Australian pelican** has the longest beak, at up to 47 cm long. #062 A flock of **starlings** is called a murmuration. #063 Before they roost for the night, starlings form huge ball-shaped murmurations. #064 Each bird tries to match its neighbours' speed and direction. #065 The constantly changing shape of the murmuration makes it difficult for birds of prey to attack any of the starlings. #066 One murmuration in Goole, in England, included 1.5 million birds. #067 Adult **sparrows** are vegetarian, but the young eat mostly insects. #068 Sparrows have been known to nest in coalmines hundreds of metres underground. #069 A pair of sparrows will raise two or three broods in one year. #070 House sparrows live mainly in urban areas but may move to the countryside during harvest time. #071 Sparrows have lived alongside humans since the Stone Age. #072 A sparrow's place in the pecking order is determined by the size of its bib (the coloured part of its breast). #073 Sparrows often steal other birds' nests rather than building their own. #074 A **wren** will feed its young more than 500 spiders and caterpillars in a single day. #075 The **Baltimore oriole** can eat up to 17 caterpillars in a minute. #076

25 FUN FLYING ANIMAL FACTS

The **flying fox** isn't actually a fox – it's a bat. It is also called a fruit bat. #001 Its wingspan is 1.5 m. #002 A bat's knees bend the opposite way from human knees. This makes it easier to run on all fours. #003 A bat's wing is so thin you can see the blood vessels running through it. #004 Bats are the only mammals that can fly rather than glide. #005 A **brown bat** can catch over 600 insects in 1 hour. #006 **Vampire bats** feed on the blood of mammals. #007 The bats bite their victims while they are asleep and lick the wound. #008 Bats make high-pitched sounds and listen for the echoes to enable them to hunt in the dark. This is called echolocation. #009 **Fruit bats** do not use echolocation but have big eyes to help them see in the dark. #010 The **tube-lipped nectar bat's** tongue is 1.5 times longer than its body. It uses it to reach into plants and collect nectar. #011 The **bumblebee bat** is actually smaller than some bees. #012 Bracken Cave in the United States has a colony of 20 million bats living in it. #013 The **flying gecko** can't actually fly, but glides using skin flaps connected to its feet. #014 **Flying snakes** glide from tree to tree for up to 100 m. #015 They flatten their bodies to catch as much air as possible. #016 They look graceful while in the sky, but usually crash-land. #017 There are about 50 different types of **flying squirrel**. #018 Flying squirrels can live for around 10 years in captivity and up to 6 years in the wild. #019 They can make 180-degree turns during gliding. #020 Thick paws help cushion their landing. #021 Ballooning **spiders** use their silk to create floating parachutes to glide through the air. #022 Parachuting is a dangerous mode of transport for spiders and is practised more by young, light spiders than older, heavier ones. #023 **Colugos** are gliding mammals that inhabit forests in South-East Asia. #024 Unlike other gliding mammals, even the spaces between their fingers and toes are webbed to increase the total surface area of their gliding skin. #025

12 FACTS ABOUT SPINDLY SPIDERS

Spiders have **HUGE BRAINS** for their size. The brains of some spiders even spill over into their legs. #001

When they are finished with their webs, spiders **eat the silk** to recycle it. #002

Most spiders have **8 eyes.** #003

Spider silk shrinks when it gets wet. This means that webs built at dawn are pulled tight by the morning dew. #004

Spiderlings fly on the wind by making **'kites'** out of silk. #005

Wolf spider mothers **CARRY THEIR YOUNG** on their backs for several weeks after they are born. #006

Female nursery web spiders often eat the males after mating with them. #008

Tarantulas can live for up to **30 YEARS.** #007

The **CRAB SPIDER** can **CHANGE COLOUR** to match its surroundings. It hides in wait for unsuspecting prey. #009

The **largest spider's web ever found** covered a line of trees **180 M** long in **Texas, USA.** #010

The largest spider in the world is the **GOLIATH BIRDEATER** TARANTULA with a leg span of **30 CM.** #011

Despite its name, the **Goliath birdeater** does not normally feed on birds, but it has been known to take **small hummingbirds.** #012

13 Bee FACTS

Killer bees will chase you for hundreds of metres if they are threatened.
#001

Worker bees are all sterile females – they cannot reproduce.
#002

The honeybee stores the nectar it collects from flowers in pouches behind its legs.
#003

The honeybee's wings beat about 11,400 times per minute, making its distinctive buzz.
#004

Honeybees' stingers have a barb that sticks in the victim's body. The bee **leaves its stinger and venom behind, and dies soon afterwards.**
#005

Honeybees visit between **50 and 100** flowers during one trip.
#006

The queen is fertilized by male drone bees. Males do no work at all, and have no sting; all they do is mate.

#007

The queen bee can lay her own weight in eggs in one day, and up to 200,000 eggs a year.

#008

The queen bee may mate with up to 17 drones over a 1–2 day period of mating flights.

#009

Bees build a honeycomb in their nests to house their larvae and stores of honey and pollen.

#010

The cells of a honeycomb are hexagonal (six-sided) in shape, and made of a fatty substance called beeswax.

#012

Bees 'crowd' an intruder to the hive in a ball of bees, raising the temperature around the intruder and killing it.

#011

During winter, honeybees feed on the honey they made during the summer. They form a tight cluster in their hive to keep the queen and themselves warm.

#013

BUGS & CREEPY CRAWLIES
FACTFILE

FRIENDS AND **PESTS**

ANTS' WORST ENEMIES are other ants. Ants from other colonies, even of the same species, are treated as enemies to be invaded and destroyed.

#001

The tiny pharaoh ant is **A MAJOR PEST** in hospitals and offices in tropical countries. It can make a nest between two sheets of paper.

#002

Aphids are tiny insects that **destroy crops** and garden flowers. They feed by **sucking** the sap from the stems of the plants.

#003

BEES are essential to human agriculture.

Their nectar gathering from one flower to another pollinates our crops.

#004

BUG **BEHAVIOUR**

Grasshoppers can **SPIT A BROWN FLUID** when threatened. This was once known as 'tobacco juice' because grasshoppers would feed on tobacco crops.

#005

The rubytail wasp, or cuckoo wasp, lays its  **eggs** in the nests of other bees or wasps. When the eggs hatch, the grubs eat the hosts' grubs and food stores.

#006

Army ants can set up **'camp'** for the night by forming **a large bivouac** made entirely of the ants' bodies.

#007

Honeybees point other bees in the direction of food by **dancing.**

THE MOVEMENTS

indicate the direction and distance to fly in to find the food.

#008

YUCKY BUGS

The best way to **remove a leech** is with your **fingernail.** Never use a flame to remove a leech. It will **vomit its stomach contents** into your wound, and could cause disease. #010

The larva of the lily beetle protects itself from predators by covering its whole body in its own **runny poo.** #011

After studying **300,000 flies,** researchers in China concluded that the average house fly carries 2 million bacteria on its body. #009

House flies are particularly attracted to **pet poo** because it really **pongs** and is easy for them to find. #013

If a fly **SPOTS** a group of flies, it will join them. That's why sticky flypaper works so well. #014

Fly maggots feed on **ROTTING FLESH.** #012

WEIRD BUT TRUE

The mantid looks like it is praying when it holds its front legs up. This led the ancient Greeks to think it had supernatural powers. #016

A scorpion's body glows under **ULTRAVIOLET LIGHT.** #017

The **LARGEST** ant colony ever found was a colony of Argentinian ants that stretched **6000 km** along the Mediterranean coast. #015

The peppered moth has evolved with the changing human environment. As pollution from factories darkened trees during the 19th century, the moth gradually changed from white to black, **to hide from predators.** #018

Like adult insects, caterpillars have just **six legs.** The rest of the legs you see are 'false legs', which they use to hold on to leaves as they feed. #020

CATERPILLAR POO is called 'frass'. It contains lots of nutrients for plants, and makes an excellent fertilizer. #019

33

58 AMAZING

Amphibians were the first animals to live on land. #001 A group of **toads** is called a knot. #002 Toads have shorter legs than frogs, so they walk instead of hopping. #003 Toads do not have teeth, but most frogs do. #004 Most toads burrow beneath the ground in the daytime and come out at night to feed on insects. #005 A toad's bumpy skin helps it blend into the environment around it. #006 Many countries have built toad tunnels under roads, so that toads can cross safely. #007 The wart-like glands behind a toad's ears are dangerous – they squirt poison at predators. #008 There are about 550 species of **salamander**. #009 Most salamanders have gills and lungs. #010 One type of salamander has gills but no lungs, so when it is on land, it breathes through its skin. #011 Male salamanders become a brighter colour during the mating season, in order to attract females. #012 Each individual **spotted salamander** has its own unique pattern of spots. #013 The **Chinese giant salamander** is the largest salamander in the world. #014 It can weigh up to 65 kg – the same weight as an average woman. #015 It can grow up to 1.8 m long – the height of a tall man. #016 The **olm** is a blind and transparent salamander. #017 It can survive up to 10 years without food. #018 The **axolotl** is a unique salamander which keeps its juvenile appearance. #019 Roasted axolotl is considered a delicacy in Mexico. #020 It is only found in Lake Xochimilco and surrounding canals in Mexico City. #021 An axolotl can regrow its limbs and tail, but it can also regenerate damaged parts of its brain and other organs. #022 Larger axolotls sometimes eat smaller ones. #023 Similar-sized axolotls eat each other's limbs. #024 **Newts** spend their lives on land, returning to the water to breed. #025 Newts can grow new limbs, eyes, hearts and jaws. #026 The **great crested newt** is the UK's largest newt species. #027 The great crested newt is a protected species in the UK, and you need a licence to handle one. #028 During mating season, the male great crested newt develops a large wavy crest on his back. #029 Newts can mate without touching each other. #030 When newts come out of water after breeding, they can travel up to 1 km on land, looking for food, such as worms and beetles. #031 Most newts have poisonous skin to protect them from predators. #032 The **Japanese fire belly newt** can regenerate its eye lens up to 18 times during its lifetime. #033 **Palmate newts** got their name because their feet look like human hands. #034 The **rough-skinned newt** produces enough poison to kill a human, but it would only be harmful if the newt was eaten. #035 A **caecilian** is often confused with a worm, but it's actually a kind of amphibian. #036 Its skin is made up of ring-shaped segments that encircle its entire body. #037 Unlike a worm, it has a skull and a backbone. #038 Some species of caecilian have no lungs and breathe through their skin. #039 They have a pair of tentacles on their face that can sniff out food. #040 Like other amphibians, the caecilian releases toxins to deter predators. #041 A mother feeds her babies by allowing them to scrape skin off her body and eat it. #042 The **Sagalla caecilian** feels its way around using the tentacles on the side of its head. #043 Most amphibians lay eggs in clusters called spawn. #044 Toads lay spawn in strings up to 1 m long. #045 One frogspawn contains about 2,000 eggs. #046 A female newt lays one egg at a time on a piece of pond plant. #047 After laying the egg, she closes the leaf around it to protect the egg. #048 Frogs, toads and salamanders start life as **tadpoles**. #049 Tadpoles live in water and breathe using gills. #050 A tadpole begins as a dot-shaped embryo inside an egg. #051 As it grows, the tadpole eats its way through the egg jelly. #052 After 21 days, the tadpole leaves the jelly, complete with gills and a long tail. #053 In medieval times, tadpoles were called

AMPHIBIAN facts

porwiggles or pollywogs. #054 As they grow, tadpoles absorb their tails into their body. #055 Tadpoles can survive for some time out of water, so long as they remain moist. #056 As they grow, tadpoles develop lungs and eventually leave the water. #057 Amphibians have many enemies, but their biggest threat is often pollution because they absorb harmful toxins through their skin. #058

44 FASCINATING FROG FACTS

Frogs don't drink water! #001 They absorb it through their skin. #002 Every frog call is unique to its species. Some sound like a croak, others like a whistle or the chirp of a bird. #003 A group of frogs is called an army. #004 When a frog hibernates, its bones grow a new layer. #005 You can tell how old a frog is by counting the layers in its bones. #006 Some frogs can jump 20 times their body length! #007 When a frog swallows its prey, it blinks; this pushes its eyeball down on top of its mouth to help push the food down. #008 A tornado can suck water high into the air. If that water contains frogs, it may rain frogs some time later! #009 A frog catches its prey with its long tongue. When it's not needed, the tongue stays rolled up inside the frog's mouth. #010 **Tree frogs** keep moist by sitting in pools of water on leaves. #011 Rather than webbed feet, like other frogs, tree frogs have sticky pads on their feet for climbing. #012 The **White's tree frog** has a tendency to get fat, so is also known as the dumpy frog. #013 The **waxy monkey leaf frog** is covered in a sticky substance to stop its body from drying out in the high trees of the Amazon. #014 Its skin contains a powerful drug, used by Amazonian tribes in rituals, that makes people see things that are not there. #015 Some Australian frogs create their own insect repellent, which smells like rotten meat. #016 The **golden poison dart frog** is one of the most toxic animals on Earth. #017 It contains enough poison to kill 10 adults. #018 But the fire-bellied snake can eat the golden poison dart frog – it is immune to its poison. #019 The **blue-jeans poison dart frog** has a red body with blue legs. It looks like it's wearing blue jeans, hence its name. #020 Poisonous frogs get much of their poison from the alkaline-rich ants and other bugs they eat. #021 The world's largest frog is the **goliath frog**, which lives in Western Africa. #022 It can grow up to 33 cm and weigh as much as a small baby! #023 The goliath frog can jump more than 3 m. #024 The smallest frog in the Northern Hemisphere is the *Eleutherodactylus iberia*, which is less than 10 mm long. #025 It is only found in Cuba. #026 The smallest frog in the Southern Hemisphere is the *Paedophryne amauensis* from Papua New Guinea, which is less than 8 mm long. #027 The **wood frog** freezes solid during the winter, but survives and thaws out again in spring. #028 **Horned frogs** have a projecting flap, or horn, of skin above each eye. #029 **Banded bullfrogs** are the same colour as the bark of the tree they cling to, making them almost impossible to see. #030 To confuse predators, some frogs have stripes on their backs that appear to split the frog in two when seen from above. #031 The **glass frog** has transparent skin. #032 You can see its heart beating and its stomach digesting food. #033 Male frogs are often more colourful than females – they use their appearance to attract mates. #034 The **large four-eyed frog** has a pair of eyespot marks on its backside that are actually poison glands. #035 Some frogs feed their tadpoles unfertilized eggs, if there is no other food available. #036 The **waxy monkey leaf frog** lays its eggs in a jelly-like substance rolled up in a leaf. #037 When the tadpoles emerge, they drop off the leaf into the water below. #038 The male **Darwin's frog** carries fertilized eggs in his vocal pouch. #039 The tadpoles develop in the pouch and, when they are tiny froglets, hop out and swim away. #040 If you show pet frogs dripping water, it might help them reproduce as they will think it's the rainy season, which is when frogs reproduce in the wild. #041 The extinct **gastric brooding frog** looked after its young in its stomach. #042 When they were ready, the young froglets hopped out of their mother's mouth. #043 Some frogs' eggs hatch into frogs with tails, bypassing the tadpole stage. #044

11 LIZARD FACTS

There are about **5000** different **species** of lizard.

#001

Lizards smell by sticking out their **tongues.**

#002

In the **BREEDING SEASON,** male agama lizards turn their heads and tails **BRIGHT ORANGE** and their bodies **BLUE** in order to attract females.

#003

When threatened by a predator, the armadillo girdled lizard **curls up** and becomes an **unappetizing spiky ball.**

#004

The bearded dragon's beard **TURNS BLACK** when it is **ANGRY.**

#005

Skinks are lizards with **short necks** and **short legs.** Some have no legs at all, and move like snakes. #006

Glass lizards look like snakes, **but they have the eyelids and ear openings of a lizard.** #007

Caiman lizards eat almost nothing other than **snails.** #008

Lizards can give a **painful bite,** but none is as venomous as some snakes'. #009

The **common basilisk** can **run on water,** and is sometimes called the **Jesus Christ lizard.** #010

Many lizards have a **DEWLAP,** which is a loose flap of skin that grows down under the chin. They use these to **COMMUNICATE WITH EACH OTHER.** #011

10 FACTS ABOUT
CROCODILES

Crocodiles can swim at up to 25 km/h. #001

They do not use their legs to swim, but push themselves forwards by swishing their tails from side to side. #002

On land, crocodiles crawl on their bellies. When they want to move quickly, they hold their bodies above the ground in a movement called a **'high walk'.** #003

Just before they hatch, baby crocodiles call out to their mothers from inside their eggs. This lets the mother know to come and guard them. #004

Crocodiles have another set of teeth in their jaws ready to replace a lost or broken one. #006

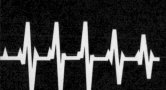

Saltwater crocodiles can slow their heart rate down to **3 beats per minute.** #005

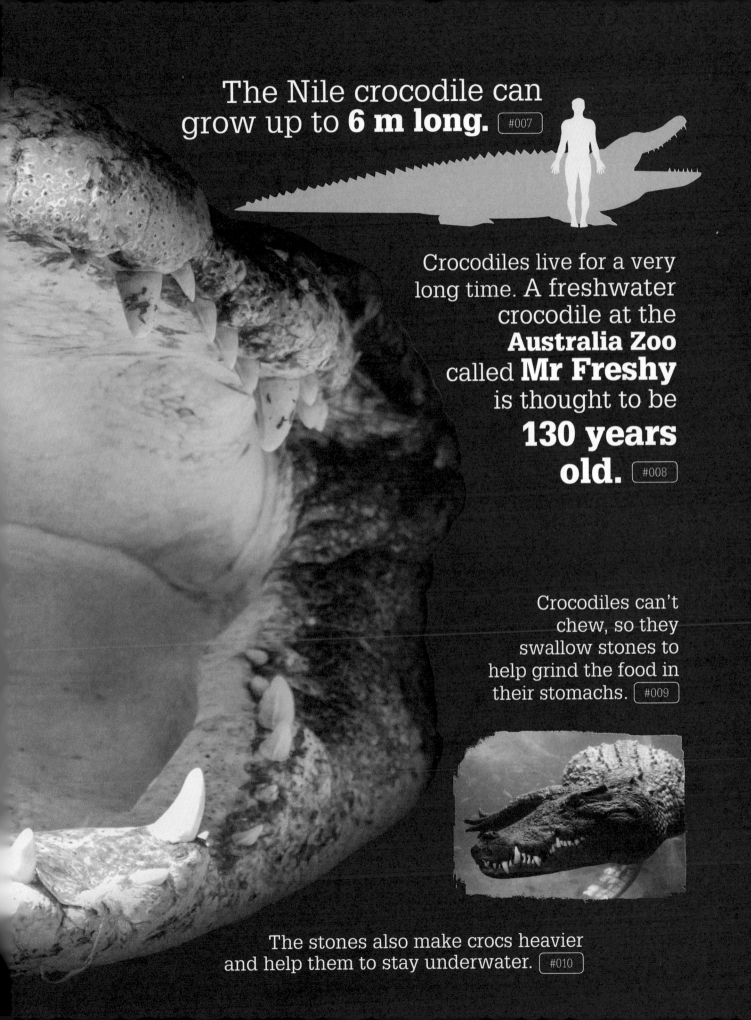

The Nile crocodile can grow up to **6 m long.** #007

Crocodiles live for a very long time. A freshwater crocodile at the **Australia Zoo** called **Mr Freshy** is thought to be **130 years old.** #008

Crocodiles can't chew, so they swallow stones to help grind the food in their stomachs. #009

The stones also make crocs heavier and help them to stay underwater. #010

REPTILES
FACTFILE

AMAZING REPTILES

Reptiles are found on every continent...

...**except** Antarctica.

#001

REPTILES do not **SWEAT.** #002

Snakes are all descended from **four-legged lizards.** #003

Reptiles are **cold-blooded,** meaning that they must warm up in the sun before they become active. #004

WEIRD BUT TRUE

In the USA, **13 million** reptiles are kept as pets. #005

Spitting cobras **squirt** venom into their victims' eyes to blind them. #006

In the USA, more people die from **bee stings** than from **snakebites.** #007

A black rat snake was once born with **TWO HEADS.** It lived for 20 years. #008

Some prehistoric snakes grew as long as a bus.

#009

The leatherback sea turtle has a bendy, rubbery shell. #010

REPTILE **BEHAVIOUR**

In order to grow, snakes **must moult their OLD SKIN.** #011

The slender-snouted crocodile is the only crocodile that **climbs trees.** #012

THE FLYING DRAGON lizard glides through the air using two large flaps of skin. It steers with its tail. #014

MARINE IGUANAS
dive up to 15 m in the oceans to feed on algae.

#013

DANGEROUS REPTILES

CROCODILES often **sleep with their mouths wide open**. This stops them from overheating. #016

About **30 per cent** of snakes are venomous. Of those, only about 5 per cent are **a danger to humans.** #015

Worldwide, 2.5 million people are bitten by snakes every year. #017

TWO THIRDS of all the snakebites on humans in Africa are made by PUFF ADDERS. #018

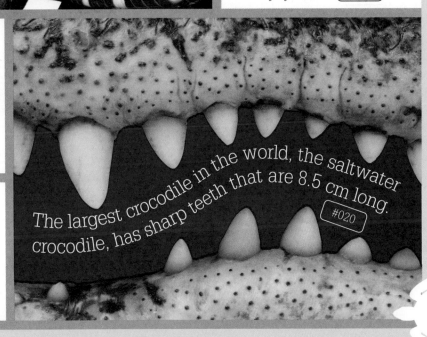

The largest crocodile in the world, the saltwater crocodile, has sharp teeth that are 8.5 cm long. #020

To scare off **PREDATORS** the frilled lizard opens a large frill on its neck to make it look bigger than it really is. #019

10 BABY ANIMAL BRAINTEASERS

An **ostrich egg** is so **strong** that you could stand on it without breaking it. #001

Mice breed so fast that in one year, two mice can multiply to become over **4,000 mice.** #002

A newborn baby **kangaroo** is smaller than your **thumb.** #003

The most **yolks** ever found in one chicken **egg** is nine. #004

Giraffes give birth standing up, so their babies fall **2 m** onto the ground. Ouch! #005

A **Surinam toad's** babies hatch out from under the skin on her back. #006

Sand tiger sharks often start to **eat each other** inside their mum's body before being born. #007

Baby **tortoise beetles** put predators off by covering themselves in their own poo. #008

Baby **periodical cicadas** can live for **17 years** underground, yet once they become adults, they live only a **few weeks.** #009

Baby **elephants** greet each other by **intertwining trunks**, and they like to play chase games! #010

6 GIRAFFE FACTS

The giraffe is the **tallest land animal**, standing as high as **6 m.** #001

The giraffe has a **blue-black** tongue that is nearly HALF A METRE long. #002

Giraffes can **run at 56 km/h** in short bursts. #003

Sometimes a giraffe will rest with its head bending back to its body. #004

To get enough blood **up its long neck** to the brain, a giraffe has to **pump blood twice as hard as other large mammals.** #005

MALE GIRAFFES fight each other by **smashing their heads** against one another. #006

43

10 PENGUIN FACTS

Antarctica

Penguins in **Antarctica** are easy to film. They have no predators on land, so they are not afraid of humans. #001

All penguins live in the Southern Hemisphere. #002

Most penguins live in cold places, but the **Galápagos penguin** lives near the equator. #003

As they swim, penguins leap out of the water in arcs — an action called **porpoising.** #004

Rather than walk, penguins slide down icy hills on their bellies. #005

The emperor penguin breeds in the Antarctic winter. The females leave the eggs with the males, who huddle together in their thousands in **temperatures of**

-50°C.

#007

The males incubate the eggs by **balancing them on their feet for 64 days.**

#009

By the time the egg hatches, the male has not eaten for **115 days.**

#010

Emperor penguins can stay underwater for **18 minutes,** and dive to depths of

535 m.

#006

The emperor penguin stands 1.2 m tall, and weighs up to 45 kg. It is the largest species of penguin.

#008

45

INDEX

A
albatrosses 26
amphibians 34–35
ants 32, 33
apes 4
aphids 32
axolotls 34

B
badgers 17
bar-tailed godwits 27
bats 16, 27
bears 14–15, 16
bees 19, 30–31, 32, 40
beetles 33, 42
beluga whales 21
big cats 7
birds 13, 26–27
blue tits 26
bonobos 4
bowerbirds 26
bowhead whales 20, 21
brown bears 14
bustards 27

C
caecilians 34
caterpillars 27, 33
cats 6–7
cheetahs 7
chimpanzees 4
cicadas 42
clownfish 23
cold-blooded animals 40
colugos 27
communication 11, 20, 32, 37
condors 26
coral reefs 22–23
crocodiles 38–39, 41
crows 26

D
dogs 8–9

E
echolocation 27
eels 25
elephants 10–11, 16, 17, 42

F
fish 18–19, 23, 24, 25
flamingos 26
flies 33
flying foxes 27
flying squirrels 27
frigatebirds 26
frogs 34, 35

G
geckos 27
gestation 10, 17
gibbons 4
giraffes 16, 42, 43
gorillas 5
grasshoppers 32
Great Barrier Reef 23
great white sharks 19
greyhounds 8
grizzly bears 14, 15

H
herons 26
hippos 12
horns 13
humans 4
humpback whales 20
hyenas 17

I
iguanas 41

J
jaguars 7
jays 26

K
kangaroos 42
keratin 13
kingfishers 26

L
leeches 33
lifespan 20, 39
lions 7
lizards 36–37, 41
lobsters 25

M
macaws 26
maggots 33
mammals 4–17, 20–21
manatees 25
mantids 33
mice 16, 42
migration 26
moths 33

N
narwhals 21
newts 34
nightingales 26

O
oarfish 25
oceans 24
oilbirds 27
opossums 17
orang-utans 4
orioles 27
ospreys 26
ostriches 26, 42
owls 26
oxpecker birds 13

P
parasites 13
parrots 26
peacocks 26
pelicans 27
penguins 44–45
pets 6, 9, 40
pigeons 27
poison and venom 17, 30, 34,
    35, 40, 41
polar bears 15, 16
prairie dogs 16
primates 5
puffer fish 23
purring 6

R
reproduction 17, 24, 31, 34,
    35, 45
reptiles 36–41
rhinos 13

S
salamanders 34
salmon 24
scorpions 33
sea cucumbers 25
sea squirts 24
seals 16
sharks 18–19, 42
sheep 17
shrews 17
shrimps 25
skinks 37
sloths 16
smell, sense of 9, 20, 27, 36
snakes 27, 40, 41
sparrows 27
spectacled bears 14
speed 7, 8, 15, 43
sperm whales 20
spiders 27, 28–29
sponges 25
squid 20, 25
starfish 23, 25
starlings 27
sun bears 15

T
tadpoles 34 35
tarantulas 28, 29
teeth 11, 12, 38, 41
terns 27
third eyelid 8
tigers 7
toads 34, 42
toucans 26
turtles 25, 40
tusks 10, 16, 21

V
vultures 26, 27

W
walruses 16
warm-blooded animals 16
wasps 32
whale sharks 18
whales 12, 20–21, 25
worms 25
wrens 27

ACKNOWLEDGEMENTS

t = top, b = bottom, l = left, r = right, c = centre

Cover images courtesy of istockphoto.com and Shutterstock.com
Back cover bl: Corey Ford/Stocktrek Images/Getty Images

4l Peter Wollinga/Shutterstock.com, 5tr Hill2k/Shutterstock.com, 6tl Maksim Shmeljov/Shutterstock.com, 7t Maros Bauer/Shutterstock.com, 8–9 Mashe/Shutterstock.com, 10–11 George Dolgikh/Shutterstock.com, 12b Stu Porter/Shutterstock.com, 13tr Villers Steyn/Shutterstock.com, 13cr Johann Swanepoel/Shutterstock.com, 14bl lighttraveler/Shutterstock.com, 15tr Molly Marshal/Shutterstock.com, 15br Erik Mandre/Shutterstock.com, 16–17 Sarah Cheriton-Jones/Shutterstock.com, 16tc Cool Kengzz/Shutterstock.com, 16tr Christian Musat/Shutterstock.com, 16bl Henk Bentlage/Shutterstock.com, 16br Iakov Filimonov/Shutterstock.com, 17br Daniel Alvarez/Shutterstock. com, 18bl Ian Scott/Shutterstock.com, 19tr Photomyeye/Dreamstime.com, 22bc DJmattaar/Dreamstime.com, 23cl Cbpix/Dreamstime.com, 23tr istockphoto.com, 24-25 Nilzer/Dreamstime.com, 24cl bikeriderlondon/Shutterstock.com, 25tr Paul Cowell/Shutterstock.com, 25cr Bozena Fulawaka, 28c Cathy Keifer, 30tl, b, 31t Eric Isselee/Shutterstock.com, 30cr, 31bl, cr Peter Waters/Shutterstock.com, 31cl Takahashi/Creative Commons Attribution-Share Alike, 32–33 dcwcreations/Shutterstock.com, 32cr Eduard Kyslynskyy/Shutterstock.com, 33tc szefei/Shutterstock.com, 33br Jefras/Dreamstime.com, 36tl Teddykebab/Dreamstime.com, 37br Leena Robinson/Shutterstock.com, 38–39c Yentafern/Shutterstock.com, 39br Netfalis—Ryan Musser/Shutterstock.com, 40–41 Olena/Shutterstock.com, 40bl Yuri 2010/Shutterstock.com, 41cl Dennis Donohue/Shutterstock.com, 41br Eric Isselee/Shutterstock.com, 43tr Colin Edwards Wildside/Shutterstock.com, 43b davidstockphoto/Shutterstock.com, 44–45 Jan Martin Will/Shutterstock, 44 Armin/Dreamstime.com